Ellis Island

TRACING YOUR FAMILY HISTORY
THROUGH AMERICA'S GATEWAY

D0376722

LORETTO DENNIS SZUCS

Ancestry.

Published by Ancestry® Publishing, an
imprint of MyFamily.com, Inc.
360 W. 4800 North
Provo, Utah 84604
www.ancestry.com

First edition published 1986
Revised edition 2000
10 9 8 7 6 5 4 3 2 1

Printed in the United States of America

Library of Congress Cataloging-in-Publication Data

Szucs, Loretto Dennis.
  Ellis Island : tracing your family history through America's gateway /
Loretto Dennis Szucs.—Rev. ed.
    p. cm.
Includes bibliographic references.
  ISBN 0-916489-95-7
  1. Immigrants—United States—Genealogy. 2. United States—Emigration
and immigration—History. 3. Ellis Island Immigration Station (N.Y. and
N.J.) I. Title.
  CS49 .S98 2000
  929'.373—dc21
                              00-011243

Contents

It is indeed a desirable thing to be well descended,
but the glory belongs to our ancestors.

—Plutarch, *Of the Training of Children*

*B*eneath the shadow of the Statue of Liberty stands Ellis Island, threshold of liberty for more than 16 million immigrants. For them and countless others whose parents, grandparents, and great-grandparents began a new American life there, Ellis Island is the symbolic shrine to freedom and opportunity. Almost half the current population of the United States is directly related to immigrants who passed through what was the principal immigrant receiving station from 1892 to 1954.

Ellis Island was the gateway to liberty for 16 million immigrants.

Give me your tired, your poor,
Your huddled masses yearning to breathe free
The wretched refuse of your teeming shore.
Send these, the homeless, tempest-tost to me.
I lift my lamp beside the golden door!

Nick Cirulli, 1990.

These lines from the poem "The New Colossus" are inscribed on the base of the Statue of Liberty. The poem was written by Emma Lazarus in 1883 to aid the fund-raising campaign for a pedestal for the Statue. A genteel lady of New York society and Sephardic Jew, she was deeply moved by the spirit which had inspired the creation of the Statue. Her words clearly define the American character and remind us of our common heritage—

that we are immigrants or descendants of immigrants. During the peak years of immigration, from about 1900 to 1914, as many as five thousand people a day were processed at Ellis Island. This dramatic figure means that 100 million Americans can trace their ancestry back to that one tiny portal.

Ellis Island reminds us in a striking way how past events influenced our lives and molded our destinies. Although we are not clones patterned exactly after our ancestors, their blood runs in our veins and we have inherited many traits from them. The character of the American people was shaped by a blend of values and attitudes brought to this country by immigrants. We cannot escape the roots of our being. On the contrary, our heritage and character have been transmitted from generation to generation, showing up in the way we think and act, even though we may lack knowledge of our ancestral history. But it is possible to travel back in time and discover our immigrant heritage.

Symbol of Immigration

Ellis Island still teems with people, but instead of immigrants, they are immigrants' descendants, and they absorb the island's buildings as if in their ancestors' shoes. They step off of ferries and walk toward the Great Hall in the same manner that their ancestors might have done. They visit the Registry Room, the ticketing offices, the baggage rooms, and other areas as part of a step-by-step tour of the process. And when they're finished, they leave with a greater understanding of why Ellis Island means so much to so many Americans.

With all of its restored buildings, memorials, exhibits, and information, Ellis Island stands today as the one of the most prominent and recognized symbols of American immigration in the United States. It was the threshold of liberty for more than 16 million immigrants. But those 16 million are only a fraction of the total numbers who have come to the United States over the years and have helped ennoble Ellis Island in American history. They are simply one piece, albeit a big one, of the larger immigration picture.

AMERICA OPENS ITS DOORS

The history of immigration spans American history. The settlements in America by Europeans in the early 1600s began a movement of people that has brought 42 million immigrants—the greatest migration in recorded history—into the country. So the story of immigration is really the story of America.

The story of immigration is really the story of America.

Students of U.S. history trace the country's beginnings to the founding of Jamestown in 1616 and the subsequent immigrant/colonizing settlements in the New England area. This colonizing continued through most of the 1600s and 1700s, until colonists decided they wanted to separate from England and started the American Revolution. Once the new country was formally established (following the Revolution), it wasn't long until issues of immigration and naturalization began to have an impact. In fact, in 1795 the first naturalization act was established, and it was followed by the first U.S. Alien and Sedition Act in 1798. These and other laws in subsequent years gave the federal government some power to regulate exactly who could enter and reside in the new country, but it wasn't until 1906 that immigration laws were made uniform. And by that time, immigration was beyond being in full swing.

The First Wave of Immigration: 1815-60

The first peak of immigration, as most citizens today understand it, began in 1815 and lasted until 1860, when the streams of immigrants dwindled

due to the Civil War. During that forty-five-year span, more than 5 million people made the trek to the United States; 151,000 new immigrants arrived in 1820 alone—one year after the establishment of the first immigration law, which required regular reporting of immigrant information to the government and which regulated steerage conditions.

(Above) The docks at Liverpool, one of the most frequented debarkation points in Europe.

(Top) Immigrant documents, including a passenger list of the Pennland, which disembarked from Liverpool.

Most of the early immigrants came from such western European countries as Ireland, England, Norway, Prussia, and Germany. After significant crop failures in Europe in 1846 and the Irish Potato Famine of that winter, many who had been dispossessed came to seek new land and a better life. Norwegians began leaving their homeland in 1825 as a result of overpopulation, and so many people emigrated from Prussia in the early part of

The most famous entry point for immigrants was New York City.

the 1800s that the Prussian government attempted to halt the flight by making it a crime to urge anyone to emigrate. But despite any attempts to discourage the move, thousands came.

To aid in processing the vast numbers who entered the United States during those years, Castle Garden, an old fort on the lower tip of Manhattan, was designated in 1855 as an immigrant station under state supervision. Castle Garden would become the precursor to the more widely known Ellis Island receiving station; it became the major receiving station of the first immigrant wave.

The Second Wave of Immigration: 1880–1917

Between 1880 and 1900, almost 9 million more immigrants entered the United States. These people made up part of the second major wave of U.S. immigration, which lasted until 1917. This wave consisted of mostly eastern European peoples, but also Asian immigrants and others. Major ethnic groups who emigrated during this time included the Chinese (who began to be excluded in 1882), Russian Jews who came to escape pogroms, and Armenian Christians escaping Muslim massacres of that time period. More than 5 million immigrants came between 1880 and 1890, and another 3,687,000 came in the decade of the 1890s.

In 1891, the Bureau of Immigration was established to federally administer all immigration laws. It was followed six years later by the establishment of the Bureau of Immigration and Naturalization. These departments managed immigration until the second wave was halted at the outbreak of World War I.

All told, the two major immigration waves brought approximately 14 million people to the United States. They entered through any of the more than seventy federal immigrant stations located along the country's shores. But the most famous entry point was the city of New York and, more specifically, Ellis Island.

New York and Castle Garden

Since it was the landing place of a large portion of the European population, New York City has always been the port of entry for by far the largest number of immigrants. Of the 5.4 million people who arrived between 1820 and 1860, more than two-thirds entered at New York. By the 1850s, New York was receiving more than three-quarters of the national total of immigrants, and by the 1890s, more than four-fifths.

Castle Garden Immigration Center, the receiving station of note during the first immigration wave.

Of course, New York's preeminence in immigration started at Castle Garden, the receiving station of note during the first immigrant wave. When the "new" federal law was passed in 1882

National Park Service: Statue of Liberty National Monument

(the regularization and standardization of immigration laws), Castle Garden continued to operate under contract to the United States government. But by 1890, its facilities had long since proved to be inadequate for the ever-increasing number of immigrant arrivals. So the government set about to build a new station.

After a survey of potential locations, Ellis Island was chosen as the site for an entirely new United States immigration station. The choice was made with the immigrants' welfare in mind. In fact, several Manhattan sites were rejected because the first wave of newcomers who entered the United States via Manhattan had been routinely and ruthlessly exploited as they left Castle Garden. On an island, the immigrants could be screened, protected, and filtered slowly into their new culture.

How Ellis Island Evolved

Although Ellis Island is only a twenty-seven acre parcel of land located about a mile from the tip of Manhattan, it was destined to become the most-used doorway to America. When native American Indians named the island Kilshk (Gull Island) after its winged inhabitants, it was little more than a three-acre sandbank of mud and clay. The Dutch purchased the island from the Indians and established the colony of New Amsterdam. It had a succession of owners before the American Revolution, when Samuel Ellis bought and linked his name to it. New York State purchased Ellis Island in 1808 and in turn sold it to the federal

Ellis Island was destined to become the most used doorway to America.

government, which wanted to build a fort on the island. Fortified just before the outbreak of the War of 1812, Fort Gibson on Ellis Island saw little action during the war. It was used primarily as a munitions depot until it was transformed into an immigration center in 1892.

Construction of the buildings on Ellis Island began in 1890. Hundreds of workmen labored to build a large, three-story reception center, a hospital for the ill or quarantined immigrants, a laundry facility, a boiler-house, and an electric generating plant. Smaller buildings included a dormitory, restaurant, and baggage station. Over the years, ballast from ships dumped near Ellis Island built it up, and the landfill and completion of sea walls brought it to its present size. When construction was completed, Ellis Island was a self-contained

Ellis Island rebuilt. After fire destroyed the first structures, the station rose again from the ashes into this most recognized form.

The second structure at Ellis Island is the most recognized.

city whose population, though transient, often numbered in the thousands.

The Ellis Island Immigration Center was officially dedicated on New Year's Day in 1892. On that day a fifteen year old Irish girl, Annie Moore from County Cork, was closest to the gangplank as it was lowered from the SS *Nevada*. She was the first person processed at Ellis Island. According to a copy of *The New York Times* for that date, "The waiting officials presented her with a ten-dollar gold piece. She had never seen a United States coin, and this was the largest sum of money she had ever possessed." Other records show that Annie was bringing her two younger brothers to join their parents, who had immigrated to New York four years earlier.

Seven hundred passengers from the ships City of Paris and Victoria were also cleared that

The Great Hall bedecked with the Stars and Stripes to welcome immigrants.

National Park Service: Statue of Liberty National Monument

day. Passenger lists for these and hundreds of other vessels that entered New York and other American ports have been preserved on microfilm and are available for those who whish to trace their ancestors' passage to America.

A Second Opening of Ellis Island

The life of the first station on Ellis Island was short. All the pine-frame buildings burned to the ground in a disastrous fire on 15 June 1897. Congress immediately appropriated funds to replace the structures with fire-proof buildings. During the next two-and-a-half-year rebuilding phase, immigrants were processed at stations in New York City.

National Park Service: Statue of Liberty National Monument

Monument to Annie Moore, the first immigrant processed at Ellis Island.

The new buildings were brick and ironwork structures with lime-stone trimmings, and the station reopened in December 1900. The main building, 338 feet long and 168 feet wide, was notable for its four cupola-style towers and spacious second floor Registry Room. The vaulted terra-cotta ceiling of the Great Hall swept sixty feet over a black tile floor which was cleaned and polished twice a day. Three bronze and glass chandeliers with hundreds of light bulbs made the room an impressive sight. The first glimpse of this scene probably confirmed the stories immigrants had heard about the wealth in America. Therefore, this second structure is probably the most widely recognized.

11

Ellis Island remained as an immigrant receiving station until World War I and processed much of the second wave of immigrants during that time. Even as the United States was tackling questions abroad through the Spanish-American War, Ellis Island was accepting a steady flow of immigrants from all areas of the globe. But with its involvement in World War I and an increased global presence, the U.S. government began to make changes that would irrevocably alter the flow of immigration; Ellis Island saw the adverse effects.

Curtailing Immigration

At the close of World War I, many Americans were eager to see immigration restricted. The war had rekindled a fear of foreigners. The Immigration Act of 1917, with its demand of a literacy test, reduced significantly the number of arrivals for a short time. However, the number of arrivals in New York soon climbed again, and 500,000 immigrants entered through the Port in 1921.

Ellis Island outbuildings in disrepair before being restored.

Photo courtesy of Loretto D. Szucs

Since the literacy test failed to stem the flow of immigrants sufficiently, the federal government enacted more powerful methods of exclusion in 1921 and 1924. Consequently, soon after the 1924 Immigration Act was adopted, traffic through Ellis Island subsided to a trickle. A final revision of the "national origins" quota system went into effect in 1929. The maximum number of all admissions to the United States was reduced to only 150,000 people annually—a deliberate attempt to set permanently the ethnic and racial mix of America.

Left alone after immigration dwindled, the facility became a crumbling relic.

These immigration restrictions dealt a death blow to the importance of Ellis Island. In its last years of operation, a portion of the island was used as a Coast Guard station and later as a detention center for enemy aliens. In November 1954, the last immigrant and the last detainee left, and the immigration center was declared surplus property by the General Services Administration (GSA). An era was over, and the once wide-open door had been unceremoniously closed.

Ghosts of Ellis Island

Ellis Island had borne the burdens, witnessed the sorrows, and heard the laughter of millions since its opening in 1892. Babies had been born, marriages performed, and people had died there. But even with so much activity in its history, once its mainstay functions had disappeared, the island was left virtually alone. It soon became an abandoned, crumbling relic. Its deserted buildings and halls, once filled with activity, were now silent—

The restoration continues at Ellis Island, and some main buildings have been completed.

alive only in the memories of those millions to whom it had a special, personal significance.

But the silence on Ellis Island could not and would not go unchecked, for its place in history had been set. Those who were processed at the island had been forever changed by their experiences there. They had taken on new identities as Americans; they had shed many aspects of their former lives to adopt American ways; and they had made it possible for their children to be born as American citizens. These experiences meant too much to the immigrants and descendants of immigrants who had come through Ellis Island. The site could not be allowed to simply waste away.

Restoration of Ellis Island

Eleven years after closing its doors, the government started to restore and formally recognize Ellis Island. President Lyndon B. Johnson realized the connection between Ellis Island and the Statue of Liberty and placed the facility under the care of the National Park Service in 1965. With this designation of Ellis Island as a national park—a national symbol—the restoration could begin.

After significant fund raising and planning over almost seventeen years, the restoration work of Ellis Island began in 1982. The restoration focused on the main island, principally the main building with the first phase of work being the renovation of the Great Hall. The designers of the restoration divided the building into two zones:

preservation/interpretive and adaptive reuse. The preservation/interpretive zone included the entrance, baggage room, registry room, balcony dormitory rooms, special inquiry rooms, and the railroad ticket office. These were thought to be the heart of the immigrant experience. The adaptive reuse zone included meeting rooms, a library, galleries, a theatre, a restaurant, a book and gift shop, and an information office. However, the Registry Room was left almost empty in the restoration, giving the crowds of visitors a chance to see the room filled only with people, as it once was.

Photo courtesy of Loretto D. Szucs

Restored buildings greet visitors to the Ellis Island Immigration Museum.

Today the restoration continues. The main building—the site where immigrants took their first steps on American soil—has been completed, but there is still much to be improved. To this end, the government announced in the summer of 2000 a new Save America's Treasures grant, which gave another $500,000 for the restoration and

Through Ellis Island, we learn what our ancestors' move to America meant.

preservation of the island's Laundry and Hospital Outbuilding. These and other structural improvements will help give visitors a complete picture of what took place on the island.

In 1990, the Ellis Island Immigration Museum opened, and it is now the focal point for visitors to the island. Its relics, charts, and displays tell again the story of U.S. immigration, as well as the individual stories of many Ellis Island immigrants. One of the most interesting features—but one that is still being constructed—will be a genealogy exhibit where visitors can search for immigrant information. Currently, an oral history center records and makes personal reminiscences available, and a film showing Ellis Island's role within the context of worldwide immigration is also an attraction. Interestingly, the number of tourists visiting the reborn Ellis Island today is about the same each day as the average number of immigrants who passed through in its days of operation as a receiving station.

Also at Ellis Island is the American Immigrant Wall of Honor, which pays tribute to U.S. immigrants by listing their names along with a copper ribbon on an extensive wall. The largest wall monument of its type, the Wall of Honor lists more than 500,000 immigrants who have entered the United States. For a fee, anyone's family name can be listed, whether the immigrants came through Ellis Island or not, and regardless of when they came.

Monument to Immigration

Now that its restoration is almost complete, Ellis Island is an appropriate monument to all immigrants. The island and its characteristic structures have been reborn through the restoration, and then they have been added to in a way that has made the island grow as a national symbol.

Similarly, through immigration to the United States, many immigrants experienced a mini-Renaissance of their own lives. They gained new hope and new direction—literally new opportunities they couldn't have discovered in any other way. They were also able to grow and progress. Clearly, their coming meant more than just a simple move; it was the culmination of the hopes and dreams of those "yearning to breathe free." And it is through Ellis Island that we learn what their coming really meant for them and for America.

Immigrants wait to be processed at Ellis Island.

THE TYPICAL IMMIGRANT TREK

For all of the immigrants who migrated to the United States, coming to America meant a long journey in several pieces. The first segment took the immigrants from their hometowns to a major port city in their own or a neighboring country; some of the largest port cities in Europe included Liverpool, England; Hamburg, Germany; Le Havre, France; and Genoa, Italy. The immigrants then boarded ships for an ocean journey that could last several months. Finally, they would be processed as U.S. immigrants in ports like Ellis Island. With a journey so long, and often arduous, immigrants needed significant motivation to complete it, and today the descendants of these immigrants seek to find out why their ancestors wanted to make the move.

Why They Came

Assessing the factors that caused one of the greatest migrations in history is difficult. Emigrants were individuals who had specific reasons for leaving their native lands and attempting to build new lives. Many Europeans were uprooted from their homes because of the economic and political changes of nineteenth-century Europe. The period witnessed the formation and decay of rival alliances and the rampant nationalism of the Austro-Hungarian and German empires; it culminated in the trenches of World War I and the Treaty of Versailles. The face of Europe was radically changed, as were the lives of its people.

This era contributed greatly to the influx of immigrants to American shores. Displaced craftsmen looked hopefully to the thriving economy on the other side of the ocean. Frequently, one who had immigrated would write or return home to tell of the wonders of "Amerika." The United States

For many, coming to America meant opportunity and a chance at a better life.

promised fulfillment
of grand dreams that
could no longer be
kept alive in their
native lands.

The lure of
America is well
known, but nearly
impossible to define.
For some it meant
religious or political
freedom; for others,

*Immigrant children learn
in an American classroom.*

freedom from conscription. But for the vast
majority, it meant opportunity and the chance to
improve their economic condition. All shared the
belief that life in America would be better.

Chain Emigration: Merits and Risks

Emigration was a common topic of conversa-
tion in communities all over Europe. Everyone
knew someone who had gone or wanted to go to
America. Success stories were abundant, but the
decision to leave home was often not easily made.
On the contrary, decisions were usually so emotional that the hopeful emigrant was torn between
family duty and his own plans for the future.

The story of Janos Szucs is typical of those
who were attracted to a better life in America.
"Our family had stayed on the same little piece of
land in Hungary for generations. My ancestors had
lived, worked, and died there. It was frightening to
think of having to leave and to break with the past

Janos Szucs, his wife Teresa Skokan and son John, and Teresa's brother Andrew.

but it just wasn't possible to survive there anymore." This same poverty had sent Janos' brother-in-law to America two years earlier. He wrote back and encouraged others in the village to come, promising everything would be better. Janos heeded the advice and in time was able to bring his wife and mother to Ohio where he had found work in the coal mines.

Chain migration patterns prevailed throughout Europe. Steamship lines and American railroad companies promoted the American dream regularly; but nothing was more persuasive than the personal accounts of friends and relatives who had been successful in their American odyssey.

Although most immigrants were eventually admitted to the United States, the consequences of deportation for those denied entry could be devastating. In the villages of Germany, Bohemia, Greece, and elsewhere, rumors had circulated about those who were denied entry because they looked suspicious or did not promptly answer the questions of immigration inspectors. The joy and excitement of reaching the "promised land" was mingled with the terrible dread of being rejected. The typical European emigrant sold his possessions and property, often going into debt to finance the long journey. He or she knew full well that deportation would mean being separated from families and complete impoverishment. For the Jews fleeing czarist Russia, the forced return could be a matter of life or death. Consequently, the rewards awaiting the immigrant to America could be great. Yet they came by the millions.

The Atlantic Crossing

The Atlantic rarely offered a smooth crossing. Frequent storms and high seas kept ships in a pitching motion, bringing miserable seasickness to all but a few. Hundreds of poorer class immigrants were jammed into the steerage sections of ships, where they spent much of the time in narrow bunks in an atmosphere tainted with disease. Separated from family, friends, and familiar sights, they must have worried about the uncertainty of their destiny during the long weeks aboard ship.

National Park Service: Statue of Liberty National Monument

Steerage passengers aboard the SS Pennland.

The last day of the voyage and the first sighting of the Statue of Liberty and Ellis Island—that last hurdle to America—brought new anxieties. Passengers of means escaped the rigors of the "Ellis Ordeal" by being processed aboard the vessel. These privileged few were then delivered directly to Manhattan. The poorer classes, however, experienced further frustration as they often

21

sat three to four days in the crowded harbor, awaiting their ship's turn to disembark passengers. On days when several large ships, each carrying over a thousand passengers in steerage, docked concurrently, the capacity of the station was woefully inadequate.

Finally, with babes in arms and children in hand, laden with bundles and baggage containing all their worldly possessions, this diverse assemblage of Old World humanity would stream down the plank and onto Ellis Island.

National Park Service: Statue of Liberty National Monument

Immigrants disembark at Ellis Island.

THE ELLIS ISLAND EXPERIENCE

The Ellis Island experience was traumatic for most newcomers, as they were closely observed from the time they set foot on the island. Inspectors looked for signs of sickness or infirmity, a limp, the empty stare of the feeble-minded, or shortness of breath as immigrants climbed the stairs to the Registry Room. Arriving in the hall, the flow of traffic was channeled through metal pipe partitions so that the room assumed the look of a stockyard. Probably as a result of that negative image, the partitions were later exchanged for benches.

The Registry Room filled with pipe partitions.

Sick, bewildered, and exhausted from the voyage, the immigrants huddled in the Great Hall of Ellis. On a daily basis, the vast registry area—frequently called the "Hall of Tears"—was filled to the walls with would-be Americans. With numbered identification tags pinned to their clothing, the immigrants awaited the battery of legal and medical examinations. Standing there today, one can almost hear the voices, in a jumble of languages, echoing from the high-vaulted ceiling.

Family members could be separated, with some accepted and others rejected. The painful decision of whether to stay or return with a loved one had to be made on the spot. For most immigrants, these hours would be the most emotional and traumatic of their lives. Some could not face the disgrace or ruin of deportation, and it is estimated that there were three thousand suicides.

A day spent on Ellis Island seemed like an eternity. What took place there was their first experience in America and overwhelmingly important. Would they be allowed into this land of opportunity or turned away at the door? From the beginning, immigrants understood that to enter the United States, two things were important above all others: they must create the impression that they could make a living in the newly adopted country and they must prove to be disease-free.

In its time, Ellis Island was a state-of-the-art processing station, but the machine was not without faults. The examinations were conducted in an efficient, but callous manner.

(Below) A psychological exam at Ellis Island.

(Bottom) An inspector checks an immigrant woman for trachoma, a contagious eye disease.

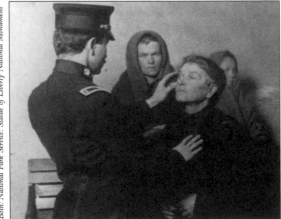

Both: National Park Service: Statue of Liberty National Monument

The first doctors made quick examinations and noted any suspicions with a tell-tale chalk mark on the right shoulder of the immigrant's usually dark clothing. People thus marked were held back for further examination. A second group of doctors looked for contagious diseases. These were the most feared on the island. Trachoma, a potentially blinding and highly contagious eye disease, was the most common reason for detaining an immigrant in this phase of the examination. The medical inspectors at Ellis Island bore overwhelming responsibility in judging the health of as many as five thousand immigrants a day. Sometimes apprehen-

sions were well-founded, but most immigrants got a clean bill of health.

Questions and Name Changes

Once past the medical examiner, immigrants proceeded to the registration clerks. "Your name?" a clerk would ask. Names were often a problem. Not all immigrants could spell their names, and baffled officials jotted down names as they sounded. Some name changes were quite deliberate. When Jan Menkalski emigrated from Poland in 1900, he knew that better job opportunities were available for German-speaking people with German-sounding names. Tracing him through Cleveland city directories and the 1910 census, we find that he called himself John Wagner. Without memories and family traditions, his records would almost certainly have been impossible to trace.

There were up to twenty-nine additional questions. "What is your nationality?" "Your destination?" "Who paid your fare?" "How much money do you have?" "Show it to me." "Have you ever been in prison or in the poorhouse?" This screening was designed to keep out the paupers, insane, sufferers of loathsome diseases, criminal,

Immigrants undergo questioning regarding everything from how much money they carry to their nationality.

and contract laborers who might be entering as strike breakers. Over the course of the island's immigration history, laws were passed that also prohibited polygamists, anarchists, and prostitutes from entering the country.

Leaving Ellis Island

Most immigrants who passed all the rigorous examinations at Ellis went to the baggage room to claim their belongings. From there they proceeded to the money exchange where marks, drachmas, lira, zloty, and kroner were traded for American currency. The railroad agent was the last stop, and here they could purchase a ticket to the destination of their dreams. Those bound for locations other than New York City traveled by barge to New Jersey rail stations. From there they entered the mainstream of America.

Photo courtesy of Loretto D. Szucs

However, many other immigrants were also detained for various reasons and varying amounts of time. Some waited for relatives to come and claim them, and others had to wait for travel funds before they could be released. Over the years, about 2 percent of the immigrants were turned back at

Ellis Island, often called "Heartbreak Island."

It was customary for relatives and friends who came to meet immigrants to bring American-style clothes, and at this point many native costumes were left behind. Would old country traditions and lifestyles be shed as easily? Answers to that question are as varied as the experiences of those who became a part of the melting pot of America. They can be found in the homes, hearts, and lifestyles of those born of this tremendous struggle.

(Above left) An immigrant woman and son upon arrival at Ellis Island.

(Above right) The same woman and son in "American" clothes prior to leaving Ellis Island.

The New Americans

Imagine proud, intelligent people, representing every country in the Old World—people with dreams -transformed through deprivation and the rigors of a long ocean journey into weary, dirty, and confused masses. In this guise they poured into America, smuggling in cultures abundant in literary, musical, culinary, and graphic arts.

One such immigrant was Giovanni Puccini, who entered the Ellis Island Receiving Station on 2 October 1902. He was struck by the enormity of the Registry Hall, for it appeared that it could have accommodated the entire population of his hometown of Borgo a Buggiano, Italy. He was

(clockwise from top left) Romanian, Bavarian, Turkish, European (unknown origin), and Dutch immigrants represent only a few of the immigrant groups that came through Ellis Island.

This page: National Park Service: Statue of Liberty National Monument

processed with thousands of others and admitted to the United States.

We can trace Giovanni's move to Chicago soon after his arrival. His great desire to adopt America as his home country is evidenced by the fact that he was naturalized in 1908—just as soon as he had fulfilled the required length of stay in the United States. His naturalization records note that two of his fellow Italian-American neighbors witnessed the ceremony as he was sworn in as an American citizen.

The greatest impression of the island comes from those who are no longer there—your ancestors.

DID YOUR ANCESTORS COME THROUGH ELLIS ISLAND?

Perhaps the most moving impression of Ellis Island comes not from what is there, but from who is not there. What befell the immigrants after they struggled down the gangplanks? Was your grandmother or grandfather among them?

According to statistics, it's likely that you may be related to someone who experienced Ellis Island during its peak. As previously mentioned, almost half of the current population of the United States is directly related to those who came through the Ellis Island Immigrant Receiving Station from 1892 to 1954. But how can you discover if your ancestors were a part of the Ellis Island experience?

The ghosts of Ellis Island were living, breathing human beings, and they are not impossible to trace. Given proper incentive, direction, and availability of records, almost anyone can follow an

ancestor's trail into the mysterious past to discover a personal family history. All it takes is a little curiosity and a desire to understand life from an ancestor's point of view.

If you have a desire to know about your ancestors' immigrant experience, there couldn't be a better time for you to start finding out and preserving this information for the next generation. There are myriad records sources, many as near as your home computer, and countless researchers who can offer good advice. These sources can help you to tap into the legacy of your own family and to place your family history in the context of state, country, and world history. The records can also help you determine whether your ancestors came through Ellis Island.

A Place to Start Your Research

The approach most wisely taken in family research is to begin with the most recent known facts and to work in a logical progression, backward in time, into the unknown. Often the occasion of a death or funeral triggers memories and questions about a family's past. The cemetery and death certificate of Elmer Johnson, for example, supplied enough information to lead to the identity of his father, Hillmer Johnson. His naturalization papers revealed that he had been born as Hilmer Kuusisto on 24 February 1893 in Kristiananstadt, Finland, and that he had arrived at Ellis Island aboard the SS *Mauretania* from Liverpool on 7 February 1917. This in turn led to the

Mauretania's passenger list, which provided an abundance of long-sought information, such as family and given name, age, whether married or single, occupation, whether able to read or write, nationality, race, and last permanent address. It also asked for the name and address of next of kin in country of origin, state and city of destination, name and address of any relative or friend waiting in the United States, a physical description, and place of birth. Thus, the search that began with a single question resulted in myriad bits of valuable information.

Begin with the most recent known facts and work backward.

Investigate Family Traditions and Home Sources

Talk to relatives, especially those old enough to remember where and when your immigrant ancestor entered the United States. The more specific the information you are able to obtain, the easier your search will be.

Almost every immigrant left relatives in the "old country," and many letters were undoubtedly sent back and forth across the ocean. Diaries or journals describing the immigrant journey have often been hidden away by distant relatives and forgotten altogether. Passports or other official documents may also have been saved. Such papers were often issued by the immigrant's home government as identification for crossing borders of European countries. All of these may provide clues that will enable you to extend the search.

Some Records You May Find

Naturalization Records. Certificates of Naturalization were issued to individuals who had completed all the requirements for citizenship. These documents were particularly important because of the accomplishment they represented, as well as their value as proof of citizenship. For this reason, they were often saved and handed down in families. Typically, a certificate will provide no more than the name of the immigrant, the country from which he or she relinquished citizenship, the date of the event, and the name of the court where naturalization was finalized. The location of the court is the key to finding additional naturalization papers which normally provide more detail than the certificate itself.

Not all aliens were naturalized; but when they were, the documentation of the process in court records can sometimes provide precise information necessary to tracing an ancestor's Americanization. Included in these records are date and port of arrival and name of the vessel on which the immigrant arrived. Naturalization laws are complicated and were not made uniform until 1906. Prior to this time, aliens could naturalize in any court of record and the information provided varied greatly from court to court, so using these records can be a little tricky. [For a concise explanation of the variation and how to use these records, consult *They Became Americans: Finding Naturalization Records and Ethnic Origins* by Loretto Dennis Szucs (Salt Lake City: Ancestry,

If they became citizens, you will find your ancestors in naturalization records.

1998), available from this booklet's publisher or at your local library.]

The National Archives and its regional branches are natural starting places for obtaining naturalization information. Major naturalization

Naturalization papers of immigrant Enrico Fermi.

Immigrants could become citizens after meeting certain requirements.

indexes such as those at the New York City, Boston, and Chicago branches can pinpoint the location of the court where citizenship was obtained. If the larger federal indexes do not yield needed information, it may be necessary to conduct a search of local court records in areas where the ancestor is known to have lived. Many naturalization indexes of both federal and local courts have been microfilmed and are available through the LDS Family History Library (discussed below). It should be noted that it was usually required that an alien be a resident of this country for at least five years to meet naturalization requirements. Frequently, the Declaration of Intention or "first papers" were completed and filed with a court soon after the immigrant arrived in this country. Logical places to look for many of those documents would be in the port cities or where the immigrant first settled.

After the required length of stay in America, the immigrant was required to go to court once more to file his or her "final papers." It was not necessary, however, to complete both steps in the same court. Many filled out the first papers in a court near where they entered the country, and then filed the final papers in some court further inland. Generally, an alien would go the the federal, state, or local court nearest home.

Certain groups of people were naturalized without filing a Declaration of Intention. Wives and children of naturalized males generally became citizens automatically before 1922. Those who served in the United States military forces also could become citizens after an honorable discharge without filing a Declaration of Intention in advance. Military records then become another source of information.

Census Records. The 1900, 1910, and 1920 federal censuses provide an indication of the naturalization status of residents, as well as the year of immigration to the United States. These records can also serve as a means of pinpointing early residences of an ancestor. The Soundex indexes to the census often will be the key to locating exact addresses in census records and can, in turn, lead to other records of interest.

A copy of one page from the 1920 U.S. federal census.

City Directories. Since a great percentage of immigrants settled at least temporarily in cities, city directories become an important factor in tracing the family. Some of these directories date back to the early nineteenth century and list names of adults who were working, their occupations, and street addresses. As with other sources, it should be remembered that directories were not all-inclusive. But although omissions or name misspellings may hinder searches in certain years, city directories are generally a most useful source for placing ancestors in a specific time and place. Directories are often found in libraries of the cities and towns where they settled. A large number have been microfilmed and are also available through the LDS Family History Library.

Miscellaneous Records. A visit or letter to the county courthouse in the area where an ancestor lived may produce a variety of records which will shed light on an ancestor's activities. At the county level, a researcher may look for probates, deeds, naturalization indexes, voter lists, tax lists, and birth, marriage, and death records. All of these may indicate an immigrant's residence soon after immigration.

Passenger Lists. Passenger arrival records are one of the richest sources of genealogical information. These records, available at the National Archives, some of its branches, and some other libraries, consist of customs passenger lists, transcripts, and abstracts of customs passenger lists, immigration passenger lists, and indexes to these lists. Passenger lists were created by captains or masters of vessels, collectors of customs, and immigration officials at the ports of entry to comply with federal laws.

They are an important resource because they document a high percentage of the immigration during the century between 1820 and 1914—the period during which most immigrants came to the United States.

Most immigrants came through the port of New York and Ellis Island. You can search the *Index to Passenger Lists of Vessels Arriving at New York* for the periods 1820-43 and 1897–1902, but there is no index for New York arrivals for the period 1847–96. An alphabetical index of immigrant passenger lists for 1902–43 has also been microfilmed. However, unless an exact date of arrival can be determined from indexes or others sources, it may take many hours of searching the chronological lists of ship arrivals to find your immigrant ancestor's listing.

For more specific information on passenger lists, naturalization records, census records, and other genealogically important collections, consult the *Guide to Genealogical Research in the National Archives* (Washington, D.C.: National Archives Trust Fund Board, 1982). Also see *Immigrant & Passenger Arrivals—A Select Catalog of National Archives Microfilm Publications*, published in 1983 or *They Came in Ships:A Guide to Finding Your Immigrant Ancestor's Arrival Record* by John P. Colletta (Ancestry, 1993).

Family History Resources

You may also want to consider getting a good genealogy how-to book. Putting a family history together requires more than just knowing that records containing family information exist. A good genealogy guide will:

- Detail useful genealogical records.
- Direct you to information sources.
- Explain how information gleaned from records can be used most effectively in order to further the search.
- Suggest solutions for problems commonly encountered in family research.
- Describe methods of recording and organizing the collected data.

TRACING IMMIGRANT ANCESTORS

What if your ancestors didn't come through Ellis Island? As mentioned, there were more than seventy other immigrant receiving stations along the U.S. coast during the height of immigration as we know it. Many immigrants entered the United States through other ports, other coastlines, or other borders. (Microfilmed passenger lists and indexes are available for a number of U.S. ports.) But no matter where they entered or how they immigrated, your ancestors' coming meant something—to them and to you. Through family history research, you can find the meaning in your family's immigration.

You can trace your family history even if your ancestors didn't come through Ellis Island.

Family History Beginnings

Begin with yourself. List what you already know about your family, beginning with yourself and working backward. Name your parents, grandparents, great-grandparents, and so on, together with their birth, marriage, and death dates and places wherever possible. Even if you have to guess at some of the information, this process will enable you to see what you have yet to learn about your personal history.

Prove it. Once you have listed all you can about your immediate family, determine how much of this information you can actually prove. Do you have copies of records? A birth record can provide evidence of an exact birth date, place, parents' names, address, ages, occupations, birthplaces of both parents, as well as additional clues that will enable you to link to other records to further your search.

Interview relatives. Speak with relatives, especially those who are old enough to remember the stories that may provide unique clues to your past. It is a good idea to take notes, or to record responses electronically. All stories are worth preserving—as long as you cite the source of the information and do not incorporate it into your family history without first proving its accuracy.

Often, the sources you have at home will contain the best clues.

Look close to home. Search for names, dates, places, and other family clues in home sources. Baby books, family Bibles, certificates, old letters and journals, deeds, diplomas, discharge papers, family photographs, insurance records, naturalization papers, newspaper clippings, school records, and scrapbooks are just a few of the sources you may find to further the research of your past. If you do not have these records in your own home, try contacting cousins—even distant cousins may have a wealth of information on your family.

Find published family material. Works that have been published by others about your family may be enormously helpful to your research. Libraries and genealogical societies have been collecting published family histories for years. Ancestry's World Tree is home to millions of names that have been submitted by individuals who may have researched one or more of your family lines. There are also millions of family-linked names to be found on the Internet.

Join a genealogical society. It is a good idea to join a genealogical society in the area where you reside, as well as in the area where your ancestors lived. Both have the potential of keeping you informed of current publications and events that can enhance your research. Belonging to a local society offers opportunities to exchange information with other researchers and to attend seminars and programs that can be invaluable in your quest. Since societies specialize in the records of their immediate area, a society located where ancestors lived may acquaint you with otherwise hard-to-find records in that locale. You may begin your search for a genea- logical society on the Internet at: <www. familyhistory.com> or by referring to the *Ancestry Family Historian's Address Book* by Juliana S. Smith (Ancestry, 1997).

The FGS Society Hall directory at <www.familyhistory.com>.

Go to the records. Your next step places you squarely in the sphere of real historical research—searching the records. Begin this phase with an examination of vital records. Most states did not require the registration of births and deaths until the turn of the century. Marriages were recorded earlier than other records and often can be found as early as the establishment of the individual state or county. Before that time, these events must be sought in private collections, such as Bible or church sources. Information provided in vital records should be studied carefully for clues that may extend the search back another generation.

Census Records

Although these vastly important records were not created for genealogical use, census records serve as an extensive reservoir of family information. A census has been taken in the United States every ten years since 1790. Data from censuses conducted from 1790 to 1920 is currently on microfilm at the National Archives, its eleven branches, and at research libraries. The 1900, 1910, and 1920 census schedules are particularly valuable for second-generation Americans because in addition to listing all family members, ages, birthplaces, and parents' birthplaces, the year of immigration and an indication of naturalization status are also provided. Personal name indexes (Soundex) are available for all states in the 1900 and 1920 censuses, but only twenty-one states are indexed for the 1910 Census.

Recently, Ancestry.com has begun putting original census records (as well as other records) online as well. As part of a project called Images Online™, users can view the original records without leaving home. For more information, visit <www.ancestry.com>.

Census records contain vast amounts of data that can help you locate your family.

Federal Government Records

In addition to the census, the National Archives and its branches have other types of records that contain genealogical information. Of special interest are military records. If an ancestor served in one of America's early wars, a pension application or other service record may supply a great deal of family data. Branches of the National Archives also have some naturalizations for the areas they serve.

Libraries, Societies, and Archives

Libraries, historical and genealogical societies, and archival depositories are all good sources for genealogical and family history data. Old city directories (which were often published from the city's inception) are usually among sources found in these institutions. If your ancestors lived in a city, it is often possible to trace their movements over time in city directories. County, city, community, and ethnic histories often include biographical sketches that generally provide personal information and the origins of an immigrant ancestor. Old newspapers are valuable sources, especially the obituaries. And archives at the state, county, and local levels are rich storehouses of original records.

The Family History Library

The Family and Church History Department of The Church of Jesus Christ of Latter-day Saints is engaged in the most active and comprehensive

Researching
your family
tree has become
even easier
with the
Internet.

genealogical program known to the world. Microfilming is at the center of this genealogical operation. Trained specialists throughout the world have microfilmed such documents as land grants, deeds, probate records, marriage records, cemetery records, and parish registers of all religious denominations. Millions of rolls of microfilm have been accumulated thus far, and several thousand new rolls are processed each month. These microfilmed records are available for public use at the Family History Library in Salt Lake City and through branch libraries called family history centers™ located across the country. The library's catalog and a number of its important databases at available at <www.familysearch.org>. The merits of this finding tool are obvious, but only a step in the process of tracing a family genealogy or history. Used in combination with the multitude of available source materials, discovery of your ancestral heritage may not be as difficult as you think.

Internet Resources

Researching your family history has become even easier with the advent of the Internet. Web sites allow users to search databases of names and information concerning their ancestors, or to connect with others who might be researching the same families. Some of the most comprehensive sites include Ancestry.com, RootsWeb.com, and FamilySearch.org.

Ancestry.com offers access to more than 600 million records in over 2,500 databases, as well as helpful how-to articles, books, and other resources online. Users can build surname communities to search for ancestors by family name, and they can post messages for other researchers on message boards and in

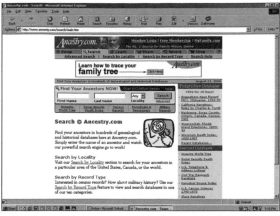

The main search page at <www.ancestry.com>.

private, personalized family tree environments called Online Family Trees. There is also a parallel search of the RootsWeb site.

RootsWeb.com has additional millions of records, most of which are different from those at Ancestry. It also hosts several genealogy projects, such as the Immigrant Ships Transcribers Guild and Cyndi's List of Genealogy Sites on the Internet, that can be extremely helpful in finding information about your family.

Finally, FamilySearch.org gives you online access to the Family History Library Catalog™ for referencing before you visit.

As the Internet continues to impact family research, it becomes less time-consuming to fill in the pieces of your genealogy. You can access many records, contact others, and learn without leaving home. And you can begin to see the context of your ancestors' lives—how they lived, why they immigrated, and what their coming to America meant to the generations that followed.

CLUES TO YOUR FAMILY LEGACY

Regardless of what means you use to go about it, each genealogical case begins as a mystery, and if the proper clues are followed, the case can usually be solved. As each new piece of information or evidence unfolds, it leads to another phase of research. Keep in mind that people and events are understandably obscured by the passage of time, and it may require more work to unearth needed information. But there are guides that will spare a researcher from many pitfalls.

Some of our ancestors were concerned only with survival and left few traceable records behind. But once a researcher knows where to look and

how to use resources to the best advantage, success is very possible. Each step of the way, history is made more personal and brought to life; after a while, it is not just a name you have found, but a person. This person may be, in some way, responsible for you being here.

As your search progresses you will realize that your ancestors were part of American history, and that you are the heir to their contributions. They were human beings. Like you, they walked on this familiar spot of ground—swayed by their own passions and moved by the joys and sorrows of their lives. They deserve to be remembered, and you are the best person to tell their story.

REFERENCES FOR TRACING YOUR FAMILY HISTORY

• *The Source: A Guidebook of American Genealogy*, revised edition, edited by Loretto Dennis Szucs and Sandra Hargreaves Luebking (Salt Lake City, UT: Ancestry, 1997).

• *Ancestry's Red Book: American State, County, and Town Sources*, edited by Alice Eichholz (2nd ed.; Salt Lake City, UT: Ancestry, 1992).

• *Guide to Genealogical Research in the National Archives*, by the National Archives and Records Service (Washington, D.C.: National Archives Trust Fund Board, 1983).

• *American & British Genealogy & Heraldry*, by P. William Filby (3rd ed.; Boston: New England Historic Genealogical Society, 1983).

• *Genealogy Online for Dummies*, by Matthew L. Helm and April Leigh Helm, (2nd ed.; Foster City, CA: IDGBooks Worldwide, 1999).

• *The Ancestry Family Historian's Address Book*, by Juliana Szucs Smith (Provo, UT: Ancestry, 1997).

• *They Became Americas*, by Loretto Dennis Szucs (Provo, UT: Ancestry, 1998).

• *They Came in Ships: A Guide to Finding Your Immigrant Ancestor's Arrival Record*, by John Philip Coletta (Provo, UT: Ancestry, 1993).

• *American Passenger Arrival Records*, by Michael Tepper (2nd ed.; Baltimore: Genealogical Publishing Co., 1993).

Your ancestors deserve to be remembered, and you are the best person to tell their story.

For a more comprehensive list of publications with specific family history information or to purchase Ancestry publications, visit Ancestry.com at <www.ancestry.com>.

Immigration 1815-1950

1815: The first great wave of immigration begins, bringing 5 million immigrants between 1815 and 1860.

1818: Liverpool becomes the most-used port of departure for Irish and British immigrants.

1819: The first federal legislation on immigration requires notation of passenger lists.

1820: The U.S. population is about 9.6 million. About 151,000 new immigrants arrive in 1820 alone.

1825: Great Britain decrees that England is overpopulated and repeals laws prohibiting emigration. The first group of Norwegian immigrants arrive.

1846-7: Crop failures in Europe. Mortgage foreclosures send tens of thousands of the dispossessed to United States.

1846: Irish of all classes emigrate to the United States as a result of the potato famine.

1848: German political refugees emigrate following the failure of a revolution.

1855: Castle Garden receiving station opens in New York City to accommodate mass immigration.

1862: The Homestead Act encourages naturalization by granting citizens title to 160 acres.

1875: First limitations on immigration. Residency permits required of Asians.

1880: The U.S. population is 50,155,783. More than 5.2 million immigrants enter the country between 1880 and 1890.

1882:   Chinese exclusion law is established. Russian anti-Semitism prompts a sharp rise in Jewish emigration.

1886:   The Statue of Liberty is dedicated.

1890:   New York is home to as many Germans as Hamburg, Germany.

1891:   The Bureau of Immigration is established. Congress adds health qualifications to immigration restrictions.

1892:   Ellis Island replaces Castle Garden.

1894–6: To escape Moslem massacres, Armenian Christians emigrate.

1897:   Pine-frame buildings on Ellis Island are burned to the ground in a disastrous fire.

1900:   The U.S. population is 75,994,575. More than 3,687,000 immigrants were admitted in the previous ten years. Ellis Island receiving station reopens with brick and ironwork structures.

1906:   Bureau of Immigration is established.

1910:   The Mexican Revolution sends thousands to the United States seeking employment.

1914–8: World War 1 halts a period of mass migration to the United States.

1921:   The first quantitative immigration law
        sets temporary annual quotas according
        to nationality. Immigration drops off.

1924:   The National Origins Act establishes a
        discriminatory quota system. The Border
        Patrol is established.

1940:   The Alien Registration Act calls for reg-
        istration and fingerprinting of all aliens.
        Approximately 5 million aliens register.

1946:   The War Brides Act facilitates the immi-
        gration of foreign-born wives, fiancé(e)s,
        husbands, and children of U.S. Armed
        Forces personnel.

1952:   The Immigration and Naturalization Act
        brings into one comprehensive statute
        the multiple laws that govern immigra-
        tion and naturalization to date.

1954:   Ellis Island closes, marking an end to
        mass immigration.